# THE EXPECTATION OF MARRIAGE

## *Helpful or Detrimental*

***Submitted BY: Cardell Mallett PHD candidate***

**Dissertation**

**Marriage & Family Therapy /Counseling**

*The Graduate College Walden University*

Walden University

ISBN: 979-8-218-09396-9

# ABSTRACT

Mallett.                                    Cardell
(Writer) Last Name.            (First)

Expectation of Marriage, Helpful or Detrimental
(Title)

Marriage & Family Therapy Counseling       John
Williams.        June 2021
(Graduate Major).                    (Research
Advisor) (Month, Year

American Psychological Association (APA)
Name of Style Manual Used in this Study


This research focused directly on the expectation of marriage. The expectation of marriage that was studied were couples view of how marriage is supposed to be. Although the study of marriage is still considered relatively new arena of research, it is increasing quickly.

The participants within this study were chosen and asked if they would like to participate. The writer spent a short time explaining the purpose of the research, the couple's responsibility, as well as what they could possibly expect. Couples were required to be married for over ten years, have at least one child within their family, and consider their marriage of having expectations. The writer then had the couples complete two questions essay separately that asked why they had expectations before marriage. This was asked of five couples which they were given the questions.

The outcome of the essays was then read and reviewed which gave the writer a better understanding about his research. The conclusion will address the value of future studies dealing with this topic.

# ACKNOWLEDGEMENT

*I would like to dedicate this to a very special man that played a father figure role in my life who showed me what a true marriage is all about Edmond Jack Lomas. He always stressed the importance of education and putting God first in everything you do. Also like to thank the many people that made this project a success. Without all of your prayers and support I wouldn't have accomplished this goal of graduating on time.*

*The couples that took the time out of their busy lives to participate in the research topic they have my utmost respect. Because they opened up their lives in a such personal way. Their stories were very exciting and informative but most of all encouraging. I pray that these couples will one day share the expectation to their children, grandchildren. Because you guys are truly a blessing for those who desire to get married and for those who are already married. The knowledge you have shared will live on through legacy of many generations. Rev Cris & LoDonna Allen, Roy & Diana Jimerson, Ricky &Theresa Franklin-Thompson, Ronald & Laurent White and Charles & Monica Handy. These couples made my research on marriage more interesting and challenging.*

*Thanks to my wife LaTasha who stood by my side when I had my surgery and through my recovery. She showed me what a good spouse in a marriage was. It is awesome how the strength of a Godly wife can inspire one to search inside oneself the meaning of dedication. Even though we are not together now her commitment will never be taken lightly.*

*Thank you to my beloved mother Dorothy Mallett who has always been the strength in my life and told me that I could do or be whatever I wanted to do. You always consider my feelings above your own and thanks for loving me when I felt nobody else did. Thanks to my other mom Marilyn Lomas who has been my tear wiper and has modeled a kind and giving heart who would give you the shirt off her back. Because of the love she has shown it has grown me to become a tender heart.*

*Thanks to my children who has truly been apart in my life and supporting and always loving me unconditionally and have inspired me to become a better person. I pray as my children get older that they will understand the true meaning of marriage. I pray for their education and whom they will encounter in life.*

*Thanks to my four best friends whom I consider brothers. When I was praying for true friends God answered with Michael Cavanaugh Sr, Mario Stephens,*

*Bishop Michael V. Johnson and Rev. Randall Carter. These guys have been there through the tears the laughter and my ups and downs you have gone through all of this with me. How can I ever begin to repay you guys for all the times you had to console me as well as listen to me complain. Most of all thank you for not getting bored with all my marriage issues. You three guys are like the ring I wear that is a circle that will never be broken and I thank God for you guys every day. I truly love you guys like biological brothers that I never had.*

*Thanks to Coresa Harris a special friend who has always been encouraging to me as I entered this journey.*

*Thank you Christina my beautiful daughter for designing my cover and being my number one fan. You will always have a place in my heart. May God bless as I begin on this journey.*

*Lastly, I would like to thank Pastor Cris Allen for his help and guidance with developing my paper. You were my sounding board along with giving me correction as well as support.*

# TABLE OF CONTENTS

# Chapter 1
## Introduction
## Expectation of Marriage

There was a woman who name was Kathy. Kathy dreamed about what her marriage would be, she dreamed about her mate would come into her life and sweep her off her feet. That he would be the provider and she would be a homemaker and take care of the kids, we talking about expectations, but she would've never imagine that her husband would get hurt at work and go on disability. That changed the family dynamic income so that caused her to get a job. Her expectations of her marriage was totally crushed. But if she went into her marriage with an open mind, her marriage would not have been detrimental.

So ask yourself is it good to have expectations before marriage because it could be detrimental down the road.

*In a relationship many people have high expectations on marriage. Some says spending quality time and truly understanding each individual has made a commitment. Some may say that having empathy to each other feeling and also having respect also plays an important role in the marriage process.*

*So I advised you to totally shift your thinking as you began to read this paper and remove your old assumption about what you thought marriage at the altar is all about and read this paper with an open mind and great expectation.*

## Objective of This Study

The objective of this study is to describe the expectations of couples who reported of have expectations before they got married. The study will constitute a qualitative format with martial satisfaction research assisting in validating the finding.

## Overview of This Study

Chapter one is an introduction to the study that gives an overview of the importance of having expectations of marriage in our today society. The objective is stated clearly within this section as well. Chapter two will focus on is it reasonable to have expectations. Chapter three allows the reader to see how unmet expectations can become detrimental to your marriage. Chapter four allows the reader to understand the fallout of having expectations and how the divorce rate is affected. Chapter five reports on putting God first instead of making expectations. It will show how important religion play in entering into marriage. Chapter six will have the reader understand the importance of having unrealistic expectations can affect your marriage. Chapter seven will conclude on the main points of the paper and will allow

the reader to decide about is having expectations helpful
or detrimental.

# Chapter 2
## *What is Reasonable Expectations*

When entering into a marriage or relationship having expectations is considered normal. Having respect for each individual, consideration for each other's differences, spending quality time with each other and understanding that each spouse will have other commitments as well as acknowledging that there will be other people in their life such as friends, family and colleagues.

Having expectations of your spouse to meet your emotional needs would be considered as wrong. The only way an individual can be happy within their marriage is to don't have expectations on your mate because you will become disappointed and loose interest in your marriage.

Society has put many variations on marriage and how we are to proceed in it, but when one let go of their expectations, they soon became happy. Because many of us may have unreasonable expectations of what life will be and how we tend to handle our chores, how much we be intimacy, how often we talk plays a role in our marriage.

Having expectations that your mate will meet your needs in a certain way, or do things a certain way, will be considered counterproductive. But that doesn't determine that all expectations are therefore bad. However, there are reasonable expectations that you should have for your spouse which are the following:

A. Expect that your spouse will fulfill their marriage vows

B. Meet your emotional needs

C. Care about your well-being

In conclusion having reasonable expectations are also unspoken. If both spouses hadn't talked about what you expect of each other within the relationship it will turn sour. When you have unreasonable expectations or not willing to meet your spouse halfway, there will be no chance for either spouses to win. Because what seems to be reasonable expectations to you may be considered unreasonable to them because there may be a lack of communication. Also you can run a risk of disappointment along with resentment when you judge your spouse on expectations that they couldn't meet or didn't realize they had. Here in this chapter you will read the testimony from the couples that participated in my research survey.

## Roy & Diana Jimerson

*My expectations of marriage and the idea of marriage were fairy tale before I was even asked. Like most little girls, teenage, young ladies, we wanted our prince who would come and sweep us off our feet and take care of us for the rest of our lives. Reality set in when my soon to be husband sat me down and told me that "marriage was not a fairy tale, you have to work at it", we have to be on the same page if this is going to work" so basically, get your head out of the clouds. I pondered on that for a few days, I remembered my mom and dad and they're marriage. I remembered there were ups and downs, but mostly happiness. I thought, I can do this, I can make my marriage last like my parents until death do us part. During the late 1990s and early 2000s, divorce was a way out of a commitment that you did not want to continue. But that's not how I was raised. I told my fiancée, when we get married, there will not be a divorce, so get It out of your mind.*

*That first year of marriage was very difficult for me, mainly because I had listened to several people who stated that the first year of marriage is bliss. We had moved to Memphis, TN, and I didn't know anyone. So, I expected bliss and when that did not happen, I was disappointed. Not to the point of wanting a divorce, but the thought did cross my mind to go home back to Chicago and regroup. Thank goodness for my sister in law, who came for a visit with my brother. It's like she knew I would need help, and she gave it to me in the form of a book; "The power of a praying wife" by Stormier O'martian. That book had me praying all over the place because when I saw the little changes, OMG! I kept praying until my husband and I were on the same page. It happened. I slowly saw our marriage become a loving, respected, committed, and communicating relationship. My husband and I were so good that we could just look at one another in a crowd and know what the other is saying. Weird right? But we were so in sync with one another through prayer.*

*I don't think my expectations were helpful, but without communication, I think they would've been harmful. Which is why communication being key to any relationship whether it be personal, or work. You need to know what the other person is thinking so that any confusion can be quickly dismissed. I'm a Christian, so I know how the enemy can work to destroy a marriage. You have to constantly stay prayed up, communicate anything on your mind; even if it's a difficult conversation, that way any expectations that you have, even after 20 years of marriage, won't be harmful to you or your spouse, but maybe you can come to a compromise in any situation so it becomes helpful to you both. I still have expectations to this day, 19 years and counting. Am I disappointed a lot? Yes, and I'm sure that he feels the same way. For the most part I compromise my expectations or in some instances, I don't expect because it may not be feasible. We can't look at other marriages and base your relationship on someone else's. That is a big expectation that may be harmful to your marriage. I remember I use to think that I wanted my husband to be more romantic and send me flowers to work as I have seen other husbands do. What I didn't expect was to find out the why husbands were sending flowers to their wives at work. So, I told lord, I am happy with who I have because I know he loves me and has never cheated on me as far as I know to this day. Those two expectations are very important to me, and was and still are deal breakers for me.*

*Again, I will say marriage is not easy. But you can definitely avoid harmful expectations through prayer, love, and communication. Be Blessed!*

## Charles & Monica Handy

*I did indeed have expectations when it came to marriage; I, like many a young woman I know, fantasized about "ideal scripted relationships" where every day was perfect, there were never any arguments/disagreements and we, as a couple were perfect in every way. Upon meeting/marrying my husband, Unrealistic Expectation (fantasy) and Reality collided. I use the word collided because in the fantasy about marriage no one was required to do any of the real work that it takes to make each day (in a relationship) as perfect as it can be. No one did anything to work towards any of the relationship substance that it takes to agree or respectfully disagree with each other. In the fantasy both people were held to an unrealistic standard of perfection which didn't allow for any possible mistakes or freedom to just...be.*

*I can honestly say a lot of the expectations that I had about marriage stemmed from books, movies and a deep desire to have the perfect opposite to the crumbling marriages my friends (and some family members) had.*

*The collision between unrealistic expectations and reality concern into marriage was helpful to me because it gave way to a liberation of sorts. I now find myself free to enjoy my marriage without all of the constricting boundaries that come from unrealistic expectations being placed on my husband/marriage.*

## Ricky & Theresa Thompson

*The expectation of marriage has changed over the last ten years for me. I was forty-one years old getting married first time for me and my husband third. I had no idea of the compromises of being married. I wanted things my way without being questioned. It was a real adjustment for me. There was someone else who had an input in the household besides me.*

*I expected this fairytale marriage. He would always make me happy, unrealistic vision of marriage. Finances would always be great. I would have the home of my dreams and a kid. Well really quick reality settled in. We had financial issues first six months due to me having emergency surgery. I had no income for three months but we survived. My father lived with us which turned our lives upside down. The fairytale marriage has faded away.*

*Ten years later deceased father for both of us. Marriage counseling on our third therapist who is the best. Communication was a big issue in our marriage. We discovered our childhood has affected our lives. We stop, listen and discuss whatever issues arise. I now understand that two people raised totally different trying to live together as one is the true compromise. Sometimes he gets his way others I get mine. We now try hard to resolve our differences in a mature manner. Listening without interruption and hearing what is being said.*

*I know that without God incorporated in our lives the marriage will fail. We study the word and pray together. We have learned that if God is not in it, this marriage will not survive. There have been times I wanted to give up. Rickey has never wanted the marriage to end and does what he can to please me. He too has realized that God is an important factor for our marriage. It has been a bumpy ride but we are riding it out together. Today, I expect good and bad days but know with God all things are possible.*

## Ronald & Laurent White

*God's Grace! I can say it is truly a privilege to kind look back and remember how far we have come as two individuals becoming a bond of one. Our traveled corridor of marriage is embarking upon thirty-six years. I honestly say that I feel blessed to share life with one I call my soul mate. I Love Ronald more with each passing day.*

*How did we get here? our initial meeting it would be described as cordial, girl meet guy. However, as we found ourselves socializing within the same circle, we soon became friends with frequent interactions and conversations. For me, our relationship began with a like and admiration before it grew into love. I enjoy the conversations we shared about life, family, work, and his declarations about being the world's best at shooting Pool. Our love was nurtured through the bond of friendship and blossomed through shared experiences both Good and Bad.*

*Our wedding was phenomenal I might add; I am still feeling at awe when I look at the wedding pictures. However, it was the after the wedding or some might say after the honeymoon that life as one became a reality.*

*Two people learning how to operate as one is quite an experience. So much we did not know about one another, the person within us is so complex and multi layered we both had embrace the good, bad, and ugly of one another face to face. It is only through God's amazing grace that we have made it this far. God demonstration of love keeps us focus on love in action. Having Jesus as lord and Savior in our lives has given Ronald and I a spiritual zeal to love and make our marriage a success.*

*Together we have gone through much, learning through the years that we are different. I would say to a large degree opposite, but time has enhanced our appreciation for one another because we learn our differences compliment or make our oneness complete.*

*Marriage is a commitment to one another. Our marriage vow was entered into freely and willingly by both parties. An oath sworn before god, family, and others to have and to hold from that day forward, in sickness and health, richer or poorer, till death do we part. All of which I find myself mentally highlighting to get me through challenging time. The foundation for our marriage has been placing our faith in God and trusting in the authority of his word. We learn through the word of God how to love, honor and respect each other.*

*What make our marriage work is our ability to live knowing there will be differences, laugh at and with each other and to love as God say love. In marriage I have learned that disagreements are inevitable, outside intrusions will come, finances and major life decisions are hurdles we had to learn to continually overcome. Everything has not been perfect; we been shaken on occasions in our marriage but our faith in God and each other got us through the toughest of times. Giving God the honor and praise for what he has done in our lives and many great things to come. Marriage is indeed honorable and bond of love fills me with joy and gladness.*

# Chapter 3
# Impact of Unmet Expectations

Unmet expectations are considered one foundational problem that is seen in marriage counseling between couples. Even though it's natural to have healthy expectations of your spouse. Realizing when we project expectations onto our spouses they are usually based on being or having insecurities as well as fear.

We can have selfishness that can cause unmet expectations. For example, wanting what we want when we want it regardless of how it will affect our spouses. Withholding information is another because which appear unselfish, this individual won't disclose their preferences or desires, this can cause resentment or criticism. Finally, being insensitive which is not understanding each other feelings and walking over them.

In conclusion, we can set high expectations for our spouses and hold to them dutifully. We may be considered a high achiever, or we may become disappointed with ourselves, and most likely with our spouses. Having a happy marriage is really about expectations tempered with reality along with a good dose of forgiveness. There are many ways we can deal with unmet expectations. For example, you can discuss

your expectations up front with your spouse, recognizing
that everything doesn't always go your way and always
be clear of your expectations.

# Chapter 4
## Fallout

Many spouses come to the point in life and fallout because of their inability to forgive the other spouse for being unfaithful. Once a problem is exposed and the behavior has come to an end, many couples tell themselves that all is well and they should simply move on. This can be somewhat misleading and considered dangerous. But what you have to remember is, it usually takes two people in order to make a marriage be more vulnerable to negative influences. This is common among spouses who have been injured by being caught up in infidelity.

Divorce is ugly when it happens between two nice couples. The idea of a good divorce is what one would call oxymoron. Whether it's the man or woman who walks away the nature of the divorce places the couples what you would refer to as antagonistic position. This will force them to look after their own personal interests.

Some people may say that divorce is a choice that most couples will regret. The most reasons couple's states that because it may devastate the children. Usually the children may become resilient and bounce back after divorce, some studies reveal that divorce leaves children with a scar for life. Even though the kids are innocent of divorce they usually blame themselves for their parent's bad marriage.

As a result, most children of divorce parents will have a higher probability of becoming abused, having difficulty while in school, and may struggle with depression.

The impact of the divorce will have family members and friends to feel like they have to choose sides, which may cost them to feel and become disloyal if they love and respect the other spouse.

In conclusion, many people believe that children will get through the trauma of divorce without any scars. They proclaim their morals and religious beliefs saying that God wanted them to be always happy. And that God is in the miracle business and there is nothing impossible with Him. And with His help, you will be able to survive and actually prosper in your marriage.

# Chapter 5
# Putting God Before Expectations

*As believers of Jesus Christ, we are called to love God and then*

*one first. The bible states Mark 12 :30 And thou shalt love the Lord thy God with all thy heart, and with all thy soul, and with all thy mind, and with all thy strength: this is the first commandment (KJV).*

*Paul tells us in Colossians 3:18 Wives submit yourself unto your own husband as it is fit in the Lord (KJV). With that in mind, the wife's first responsibility is to God and then her husband. For example, if a person is married, spouses should come next in the order as God has prioritized it to be. A man should love his wife as Jesus loved his church. This natural order is familiar in relationship that a husband should follow God first and his wife second. History let us know that the woman was created for the man and that God made her for his companionship and this was considered the first union of marriage.*

When you put God first, you have to let go of your expectations and follow your heart. That means letting go of what others people think. Putting God first will allow you to have a voice in your marriage that will allow you to become true to yourself. However, many of us don't feel that we are free because we allow living in self-imposed chains because of the fact we haven't put God first.

There's nothing wrong with the aspect of putting God first, because it's biblical. Everyone has expectations in how we would like our marriage to be, putting God first means that we give God priority over our marriage. Making him the main principal figure in our marriage. When we choose to put God first, we make Him more important than anything else. Putting God before expectations means that we keep ourselves free from idolatry. Putting God first means that we strive to make our marriage as God designed it to be. Putting God first in your marriage will allow you to be an example to other couples who are struggling within their relationship. Also by putting God first your marriage can become easier when truly following and study His word.

God has only one expectations of us and that is to live our life as one of His disciple. But for some reason, we began to develop false expectations which we place on ourselves or we allow other to.

In conclusion, society will try to tempt you within your marriage, but we must remember and understand that our identity comes from people, and that's why putting God first and allowing your expectations to be placed on Him will guarantee you a successful marriage.

If both spouses are believers, then you will automatically pray together. Even though they are one flesh, they are still responsible for their own salvation. Even though we grow at different paces, and may not always pray together the desire is there. Pray together with your spouse is considered a form of intimacy which can be more physical than getting together.

# Chapter 6
# *Unrealistic Expectations That Can Destroy Your Marriage*

This year Jim and Kathy will be celebrating 30 years of marriage. Where does time go? Jim stated when we said our vows at the alter those years ago, we were young, happy and idealistic. We meant every word we said, but we had no clue how those words would play out over the years. We went through premarital counseling and had the necessary conversations. We even spoke to our pastor periodically for additional insight. As we continued to evolve yet stick to each other through thick and thin, it became apparent how the rose- colored glasses of unrealistic expressions could drain a marriage.

Having expectations within your marriage is not bad, but making your expectations your reality without considering your reality can become detrimental. In your mind, your expectations are valid and may be considered reasonable. Knowing that your expectations don't only involve you but other around you as well.

Having unrealistic expectations won't really destroy your marriage unless you allow them to, but they can have a damaging impact on your marriage if you allow yourself to be a prisoner to your expectations. But you can turn it over to God and allow Him to mold your marriage into realistic expectations. By doing this you would allow Him to provide you with the clarity and wisdom in place of your expectations. Wisdom has taught that the best antidote for unreasonable expectations is prayer.

In conclusion, although you are married, your spouses can't be everything to you, simply because we're not wired that way. If you are depending upon your spouse more than they can handle and not God, you are setting yourself up for unrealistic expectations.

Your mate can make you happy and can probably at one time for fill your every wish you may have, but putting your happiness will be considered unrealistic because even they can have a bad day or say something that might or will upset you and now your spouse has made you mad therefore your expectations has truly become unrealistic.

When you begin to start experiencing problems, you start assuming your marriage is hopeless and avoid working on your situation or seeking professional counseling. As the result of this your marriage will deteriorate and will probably end. However, relationship is somewhat difficulty and requires efforts and compromise even when things are going good.

# *Chapter 7*
# *Treatment*

When working with couples as therapist/counselor we work with trying developing positive communication and relational skills to increases closeness, effectively adjust to life's challenges, and manage stress, anxiety and depression.

As a therapist/ counselor with creativity and warmth we like to work with clients to help facilitate personal growth to help navigate on what can be often confusing world. Together doing counseling we will increase your self-awareness, support you in finding the best and important answers to help you with life changing questions, and will guide you to have a move enjoyable and smooth life.

Many therapists/ counselor have tried many different kinds of methods to use but the most effective-genuinely and helpful are **Emotionally Focused Couples Therapy.** Also Psychotherapy which focuses only <u>improving</u> their communication and conflict resolution skills. Most personal and family relationship can be both fulfilling and challenging. The purpose is to understand yourself-your emotions and behaviors; the reason is to better you can communicate with love ones including your mate. It is very important that both parties attend marriage and together. Usually both spouses attend the sessions together, however some therapist may have the couples to be seen separately sometimes too.

In order for counseling to work both parties must be fully committed to the treatment. But the good thing about marriage counseling is that it can deal with a variety of life issues that can and will affect the marriage such as death in the family, a tragedy in the family such as a chronic illness. But the main purpose of marriage counseling is help them learn how to strengthen their marriage.

In conclusion, marriage has been known to be one of the most monumental relationship one will ever have in your life. But it's important to always be realistic. The important thing is to remember that all marriage will have its ups and downs.

# Chapter 8
# Conclusion

*Time has bought many changes within the institution of marital bliss. Within each century many writers have expressed their opinion about marriage and the expectation of the union. Marriage has been kind of understood in many terms as why two individuals decide to take that step, some say for social, or political conquer and economic reasoning which took the place of romantic love which is usually the main reason. But having romantic love in today marriage is and always should be important in today's society. With the changing reasoning why people take the step is because they have realized how much important romantic and love has become. The purpose of this research is to look at the expectation of what a couple have before going into marriage and to see if their expectation was warranted and did their expectation enhanced or make their marriage unrealistic.*

*When looking at the expectation of a good marriage, many scholar's writers' in society today say that there is a lot of confusion in the language and terminology of what really constitutes a good marriage. Bellah, Madsen, Sullivan, Swidler & Tipton (1985). states that we seem to have lost our vocabulary for formulating a common standard for defining better or worse ways of living, each individual is left to define good for himself/ herself. And with that in mind there is an expectation of good showing up in their marriage. Which can be backed up by the variable that allows most couples and will lead to excellent marital success.*

*Although marriage is one institution that many people enter into on they own free will but has a lot of personal expectation. Nearly 90 percent of adults many at least once in their lifetime enter into marriage (Schoen & Weinick, 1993). Even though the marriage rate is high, the divorce rate is staggering at an all-time low.*

*So as you have read this dissertation keep an open mind of the importance of marriage in our society today and the expectations that comes along with it.*

# BIBLIOGRAPHY

Bellah, Madden, Sullivan, ect. (1985). The expectation of marriage. Marriage &Family Review 11,129-131

Blair, SL (1993). Family & perception among husbands and wives. Journal of Family Issues 6, 331-345.

Cox, MJ. (1999). Martial perception. Journal of Marriage & the Family.61(3), 611-626

Holy Bible (KJV)

Schoen, & Weinick (1993). God and expectations. Journal of Marriage & Religion 45(5), 45-52